Happy Birthday
Cousin!

DEAREST COUSIN,
YOU ARE THE BIRTHDAY GIRL!

PARTY TIME!

COUSIN,
LET'S CELEBRATE!

TODAY IS THE DAY TO BE HAPPY!

COUSIN,
YOU ARE AMAZING!

Cheers!

FABULOUS COUSIN, IT'S YOUR SPECIAL DAY!

HIP! HIP! HOORAY!

COUSIN,
IT'S YOUR BIRTHDAY!
MAKE A WISH!

Believe in Magic!

SWEET COUSIN, YOU ARE AWESOME!

HAPPY
BIRTHDAY

HAPPY BIRTHDAY COUSIN!
COLORING CARD
Copyright 2018
By Florabella Publishing, LLC
florabellapublishing@yahoo.com